Introduction

Some people might presume ikebana, or
Japanese flower arranging, is an art from the
Old World restricted by rules. In this book,
however, I suggest a new aspect of ikebana
so that you can enjoy natural beauty of flowers
in the most simplified styles, still based on our tradition.
The examples in this book are versatile
and changeable to complement any setting.
I hope you will be inspired to be more adventurous
in expressing yourself with flowers.

Profile of the author, Reiko Takenaka

1958 Accepted at Sogetsu School.
1975 Received "Sofu Award."
1979 Received "Shoreisho Award."
1983 Received "Maxim Award" from Pierre Cardin,
France.
1985 Began providing ikebana classes at Hanamo,
Tokyo.
1988 Guest exhibitor at Ikebana International Tokyo
Branch.
1990 Held solo exhibition, "Installation of Plants."
1991 Received "Annual Award for Display Design '92"
with "Sopra Fume" installation.
1992 Designed exhibition sites for "International Jew-
elry Exhibition", "Sky Resort Show", etc.
1993 Gave lessons at "Tokyo Green Festival."
1994 Entered "Rose Festival" at Portland, Oregon, U.S.
1995 Gave demonstration of display at the Toshiba
Booth for "Beijing International Medical Instru-
ments Exhibition." Published "Japanese Flower
Arrangement IKEBANA" from JOIE, INC.
1996 Published "ENCHANTING IKEBANA" from JOIE,
INC.

She has designed and arranged numerous displays
for various events, and has given ikebana demonstra-
tions before state guests from all over the world. Now
she plays an active part in both domestic and international scenes of cultural exchanges as a promising
ikebana artist in such cities as New York, San Fran-
cisco. Hong Kong, Geneva, Singapore, and Malaysia.

CONTENTS

EVERYDAY ARRANGEMENTS

Brilliance of yellow

This is a duet of yellow flowers with contrasting textures. A lovely, modern mood is achieved by the removal of fussy leaves.

Method

1

REMOVE leaves of mimosa completely by hand.

2

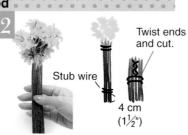

Stub wire

Twist ends and cut.

4 cm (1½")

BIND 18 daffodils by winding the wire 2-3 times at two points; twist ends.

3

STAND daffodils upright in the center of container.

4

ADD mimosa (C) to the left side of daffodils, showing the best of its shape.

5

COVER the base of daffodils by placing mimosa (A) in the front. Place mimosa (B) behind so as to add depth.

✽Hint

A thinly stemmed tiny flower, such as daffodil here, can look robust and impressive by gathering a bunch.

Flowers & Foliage

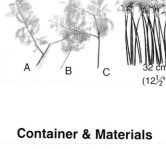

Mimosa   Daffodil

A   B   C   32 cm (12½")

Container & Materials

Glass bowl, 9 cm (3½") high,
12 cm (4¾") across
Kenzan (needlepoint holder)
Stub wire

Finished Size

height: 40 cm (16")   depth: 38 cm (15")

width: 40 cm (16")

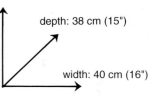

◆Variation

A gerbera is used here in place of daffodil to enjoy a balance of parallel vertical and curvy lines.

Finished Display

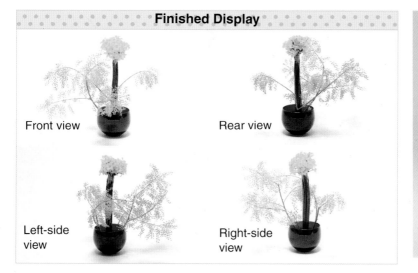

Front view   Rear view

Left-side view   Right-side view

Breeze & blossoms

A variety of flowers are enhanced and unified by the free, airy lines of cattail leaves which create a cool atmosphere.

Flowers & Foliage

48 cm (19") Cattail leaves
Freesia
Baby's breath
Statice
Oriental hybrid lily
※ Curly fern
Pincushion flower

※ Limonium blue fantasia

Containers

Miniature bottles, 2 tall (16.5 cm/6½"), 3 low (13 cm/5"), all 1.5 cm (½") across rim

Finished Size

height: 67 cm (26")

depth: 18 cm (7")

width: size of window

✳Hint

Choose the best combination of the flowers and bottles. Shape cattail leaves so as to give a soaring and naturally blown look.

Method

1 DECIDE where to place the arrangement and position all the bottles. Put each flower, facing toward you, in a bottle of watching shade.

2 ADD depth and dimension: Insert baby's breath into the green bottle. Add fronds of fern to both green and red bottles extending to sides.

3 ADD limonium blue fantasia in the navy bottle, and place to the left of the farthest bottle to the right.

4 GIVE height and movement with cattail: insert several leaves into each bottle, except one.

The green hues

Simple yet expressive lines and shades are arranged in a used bottle. Try to be bold.

Flowers & Foliage

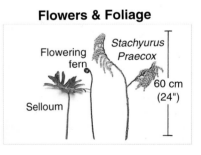

Flowering fern

Stachyurus Praecox

Selloum

60 cm (24")

Method

1 CHOOSE the best angle to show the lines of *Stachyurus Praecox*, and stand it upright so its cut edge settles on the bottom of the container.

2 ADD flowering fern to the front of *Stachurus Praecox*, aligning the lower stems.

3 GIVE depth by inserting selloum upright, its tip pointing to the upper right.

Container

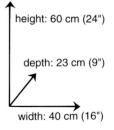

Bottle, 23 cm (9") high, 4 cm (1½") across rim

Finished Size

height: 60 cm (24")

depth: 23 cm (9")

width: 40 cm (16")

*Hint
Simplify stem lines to emphasize the beauty of green hues.

5

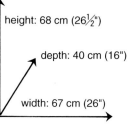

GALERIE BEYELER BASEL

Flinging branch

Few materials often say more than too many.

*Hint

Show the strength of the natural branch of flowering quince by trimming away unnecessary twigs.

Flowers & Foliage

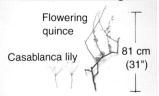

Flowering quince

Casablanca lily

81 cm (31")

Container

Assymetrical vase, 14 cm (5½") high, 28 cm (11") wide, 7 cm × 3 cm (2¾" × 1⅛") across opening

Finished Size

height: 68 cm (26½")

depth: 40 cm (16")

width: 67 cm (26")

Method

1

SIMPLIFY the lines by cutting off unnecessary twigs. Choose the best angle of the branch. Cut the end so as to fit the inner curve of container.

2

HOLD the branch so that its cut edge touches the inside of the container, and bring the top towards the back left until it touches the rim of the container.

3

HIDE the opening of container by adding 2 lilies, each facing a different direction.

Tulip trio

Enjoy playful shapes using dwarf tulips and grasstree that cascade into the other containers.

Flowers & Foliage

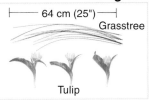

⊢—— 64 cm (25") ——⊣

Grasstree

Tulip

Containers

Glass candlesticks,
8 cm (3") and 5 cm (2") high,
2.5 cm (1") each across rim

Finished Size

height: 33 cm (13")

depth: 10 cm (4")

width: 50 cm (20")

Method

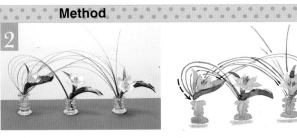

1 DECIDE the location, and position the containers at an interval. Place tulips, slanting each to the right.

2 ADD grasstree to each container. Insert tips of grasstree into the other containers; center and right into the left container, left into the center one, as illustrated.

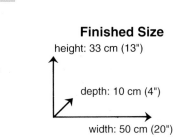

✳Hint
A few flowers can create an expressive form and rhythm as in this arrangement.

7

◆**Variation**

Flowing lines of spirea are cut short so as to emphasize the height of the tulips here. Uncomplicated curves of spirea express a light movement.

Contrast of lines

Show an unexpected contrast of curvy and straight lines.

Finished Display

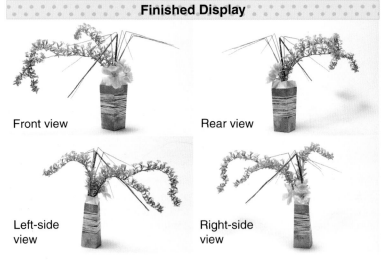

Front view

Rear view

Left-side view

Right-side view

How to make a container from a milk carton

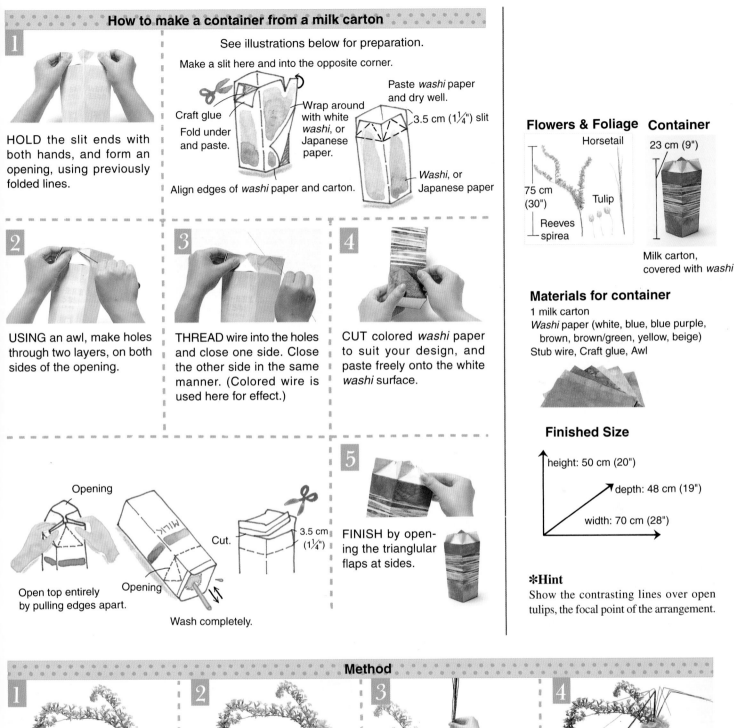

1 HOLD the slit ends with both hands, and form an opening, using previously folded lines.

See illustrations below for preparation.

Make a slit here and into the opposite corner.

Craft glue
Fold under and paste.

Wrap around with white *washi*, or Japanese paper.

Align edges of *washi* paper and carton.

Paste *washi* paper and dry well.

3.5 cm (1¼") slit

Washi, or Japanese paper

2 USING an awl, make holes through two layers, on both sides of the opening.

3 THREAD wire into the holes and close one side. Close the other side in the same manner. (Colored wire is used here for effect.)

4 CUT colored *washi* paper to suit your design, and paste freely onto the white *washi* surface.

Opening

Open top entirely by pulling edges apart.

Opening

Cut.

3.5 cm (1¼")

Wash completely.

5 FINISH by opening the triangular flaps at sides.

Flowers & Foliage

Horsetail

75 cm (30")

Tulip

Reeves spirea

Container

23 cm (9")

Milk carton, covered with *washi*

Materials for container

1 milk carton
Washi paper (white, blue, blue purple, brown, brown/green, yellow, beige)
Stub wire, Craft glue, Awl

Finished Size

height: 50 cm (20")
depth: 48 cm (19")
width: 70 cm (28")

*Hint

Show the contrasting lines over open tulips, the focal point of the arrangement.

Method

1 SET spiraea to flow naturally towards the left.

2 HIDE the opening of the container by adding tulips.

3 STAND horsetail upright. Bend horsetail stalks at the same height as the spiraea.

4 GIVE depth by spreading the stalks in several directions.

Bold and beautiful
Large amarylis flowers create a dramatic focal point in your home.

◆Variation

If making a smaller arrangement, team with airy materials such as fennel.

Flowers & Foliage

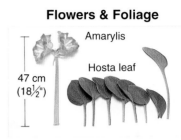

Amarylis

Hosta leaf

47 cm
(18½")

Container & Materials

Metal container, 9 cm (3½") high,
9 cm (3½") across
Kenzan (needlepoint holder)
Stub wire

Finished Size

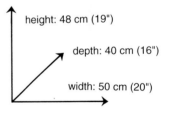

height: 48 cm (19")

depth: 40 cm (16")

width: 50 cm (20")

Method

1

BIND hosta leaves. Hold 4 leaves and slightly slide each. Bind with wire.

2

CHECK the shape so the leaves extend naturally.

3

STAND amarylis securely in the center of the container.

4

ADD hosta leaves. Set the longest hosta on the left side, slanting towards left. Secure bound leaves extending towards right.

5

ADD depth with remaining leaves set to the back and front.

✳Hint

Amarylis is a heavy-headed with a soft, hollow stem, and should be balanced upright. Create a movement by changing directions of hosta leaves.

Wipe leaves with a wet cloth before arranging.

Sunshine in your home

Express freedom and ease everyone's mind.

Flowers & Foliage

13 cm (5")

Sunflwer

Containers

Wine glass, 13 cm (5") high,
        8 cm (3") across rim
Liqueur glass, 10 cm (4") high,
        4.5 cm (1½") across rim

Finished Size

height: 25 cm (10")

depth: 15 cm (6")

width: 30 cm (12")

✲Hint
Emphasize the bright color and shape,
to make a pleasant mood.

Method

1

REMOVE petals carefully
from the smallest sunflower.

2

SET two sunflowers of
different heights in a larger
glass, each facing a different
direction.

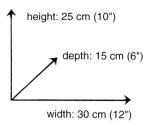

3

PLACE a smaller glass on
the right and put in the
smallest flower, facing
towards you.

Method

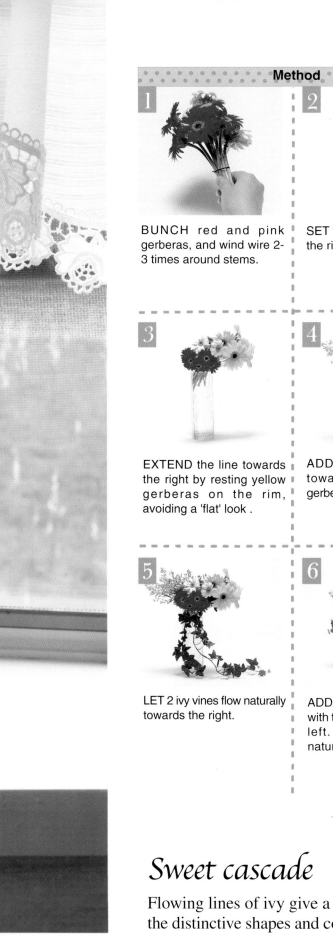

1 BUNCH red and pink gerberas, and wind wire 2-3 times around stems.

2 SET the bunch to brim over the rim of the container.

3 EXTEND the line towards the right by resting yellow gerberas on the rim, avoiding a 'flat' look.

4 ADD solidaster, fanning towards left behind the gerberas.

5 LET 2 ivy vines flow naturally towards the right.

6 ADD remaining ivy to sides, with the shortest vine on the left. Let vines cascade naturally.

Flowers & Foliage

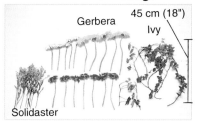

Gerbera
Ivy
45 cm (18")
Solidaster

Container

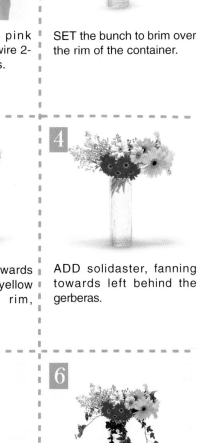

Glass vase,
25 cm (10") high,
8 cm (3") across
Stub wire

Finished Size

height: 40 cm (16")

depth: 25 cm (10")

width: 45 cm (18")

Finished Display

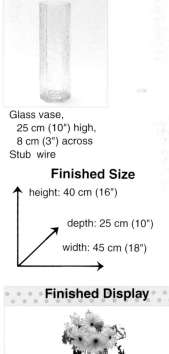

This is a right-side view to show how yellow gerberas face to the right.

Sweet cascade

Flowing lines of ivy give a delicate mood to the distinctive shapes and colors of gerberas.

✱Hint
Contrast the solid volume of gerberas with the playful lines of ivy.

Hint of wilderness

Design your own image of late summer.

*Hint

Let rosehip branch rest on the tabletop since the heads are heavy and unstable.

Flowers & Foliage

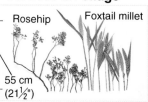

Rosehip   Foxtail millet

55 cm (21½")

Container & Materials

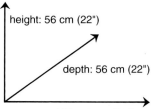

Hat
Clear plastic or glass container,
2.5 cm (1") high, 10 cm (4") wide, 9 cm (3½") deep
Kenzan (needlepoint holder)

Finished Size

height: 56 cm (22")

depth: 56 cm (22")

width: 70 cm (28")

Method

1 SECURE the longest branch of wild rosehip as if it were growing towards the left out of the hat.

2 GIVE depth to the base by adding the remaining rosehip twigs.

3 STAND the longest foxtail millet upright, then the second longest to its front. Add shorter ones to the left and front, slanting so as to echo the rosehip.

4 FINISH by adding remaining foxtail millet so as to bow forward naturally.

Flowers & Foliage

Chinese lantern

White feverfew

53 cm (21")

Daring and delicate

The bold form of Chinese lantern and a naive mass of flowers complement each other, creating a vivid impression.

Container

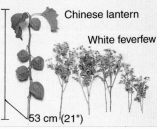

Small pitcher, 18 cm (7") high,
9 cm (3½") across rim

Method		Finished Display

1

2

SLANT a thick branch of Chinese lantern towards the left, resting on the rim of the container.

ADD white feverfew to give depth and dimension as shown.

Right-side view

Finished Size

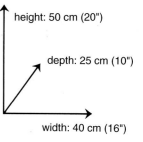

height: 50 cm (20")

depth: 25 cm (10")

width: 40 cm (16")

✻Hint
Emphasize the beauty of fruits by plucking leaves around them.

Flowers & Foliage

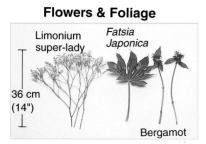

Limonium super-lady

Fatsia Japonica

36 cm (14")

Bergamot

Container

Potpourri pot, 6 cm (2¼") high, 6 cm (2¼") across

Finished Size

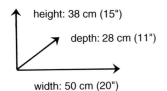

height: 38 cm (15")

depth: 28 cm (11")

width: 50 cm (20")

✳Hint
Emphasize the ascending and extending lines of the stem. Be sure to balance well since the heads are heavy.

Salutation

A stark form arises from a potpourri pot.

1 FAN out limonium super-lady, putting through the holes of the container.

2 STAND the *Fatsia Japonica* upright in the front.

3 ACCENT with bergamot flowers stood upright, at slightly varying heights.

Stunning colors

Strong, vivid shades of flowers can brighten up any dark corner of your house.

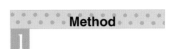

Method

1

SLANT anthurium towards the front right, resting its stem on the rim of the container.

2

FILL with stokesias, slanting forward.

✽Hint
Make it simple when using sharp colors.

Flowers & Foliage

Stokesia   Anthurium

22 cm (8½")

Container   **Finished Size**

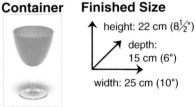

height: 22 cm (8½")

depth: 15 cm (6")

width: 25 cm (10")

Wineglass, 13 cm (5") high,
8 cm (3") across rim

Flowers & Foliage

Cyperus

42 cm (16½")

Hibiscus

Containers

2 glass vases, each 10 cm (4") high,
1.5 cm (½") across rim

Finished Size

height: 38 cm (15")

depth: 45 cm (18")

width: 80 cm (31")

A little drama

An artistic form of the grass defines the shape and color of hibiscus, which blooms only for a day.

Method

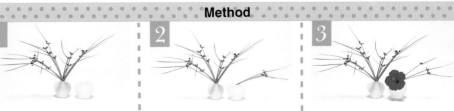

1

SPREAD out cyperus grass to the left and right, crossing the stems at the rim of one container.

2

ECHO with remaining 3 cyperus slanting towards the right in the other container set on the right.

3

FINISH with the short-cut hibiscus flower facing toward you.

Nice and cool

It is fun to create a refreshing display using everyday containers like these.

✻Hint
Express a rhythm with foliage, and emphasize the beauty of water that reflects light.

Flowers & Foliage

Billberry
Lily
23 cm (9")
Trachelium

Containers

3 baking dishes, 3 cm–7 cm (1⅛"–2¾") high,
15 cm–19 cm (6"–7½") across

Finished Size

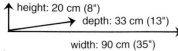

height: 20 cm (8")
depth: 33 cm (13")
width: 90 cm (35")

20

Method

1 CHOOSE a spot for the arrangement. Set 3 containers filled with water. Place the billberry twigs so that the longest ones spread to both sides.

2 FORM a light "bush" in each container with the remaining billberry twigs.

3 ENRICH the pink tones with trachelium placed only in the middle and right containers.

4 REST a lily in each container, in varying directions.

Simply beautiful

Sleek line of green goddess is emphasized with fluffy, grouped flowers.

✳Hint
Secure green goddess by trimming the thick stem diagonally and settling the edge at the inside of container.

Flowers & Foliage

Prairie gentian
(double-flowering)

43 cm
(17")

Green goddess

Container & Materials

Decorative drinking glass, 8 cm (3") high
8 cm (3") across

Stub wire

Finished Size

height: 25 cm (10")

depth: 25 cm (10")

width: 48 cm (19")

Method

BUNDLE prairie gentians securing with wire wound 2-3 rounds.

FILL the opening of the container with the bunch.

PLACE longer green goddess so its stem rests on the rim and extends towards left, the head slightly above the container. Add short cut green goddess, facing a different direction.

21

Fruits & flowers

These edible ornaments are displayed to look and smell nice from all directions.

*Hint

Use your own selection of seasonal fruits, based on the shade, shape, and size of each one. Wash flowers in water, and insert into fruits.

Flowers & Foliage

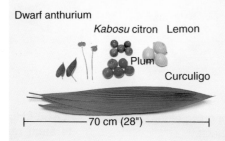

Dwarf anthurium

Kabosu citron   Lemon

Plum

Curculigo

⊢――――― 70 cm (28") ―――――⊣

Method

Layer 3 curculigo leaves, slightly sliding each end askew. Place washed fruits and/or vegetables in a good balance. Accentuate with anthuriums inserted into soft fruits.

Finished Size

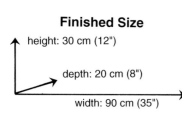

height: 30 cm (12")

depth: 20 cm (8")

width: 90 cm (35")

From jade to coral

Enjoy the changing shades of fresh cherry tomatoes set off by a groomed frond of fern that provides a sense of movement.

Finished Size

height: 20 cm (8")

depth: 15 cm (6")

width: 23 cm (9")

Flowers & Foliage

23 cm (9")

Cherry tomato on vine

Fern

Container

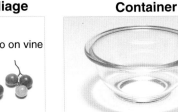

Glass bowl, 8 cm (3") high, 15 cm (6") across rim

✳Hint
Do not fill the container. Leave some space and stack up tomatoes.

Method

Place tomatoes at one side of the container so the vine stands as shown. Trim away the lower leaves of the fern, and insert at a slant pointing to the opposite direction.

Naturally beautiful

Recreate a natural landscape in your tiny container with the addition of a wild vine.

Flowers & Foliage

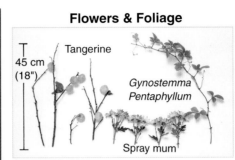

45 cm (18")

Tangerine

Gynostemma Pentaphyllum

Spray mum

Container & Materials

Basket, 20 cm (8") high including handle, 13 cm (5") across
Kenzan (needlepoint holder)
Inner container

Finished Size

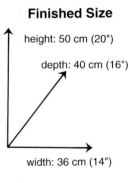

height: 50 cm (20")

depth: 40 cm (16")

width: 36 cm (14")

Finished Display

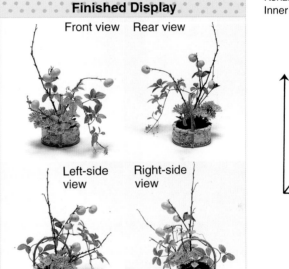

Front view   Rear view

Left-side view   Right-side view

◆**Variation**

Foxface, tall eucalyptus, and rising gerberas are arranged to capture the feeling of a forest of early autumn.

✳**Hint**

In order to set off the fruit, trim away unnecessary leaves and check the overall balance carefully.

Method

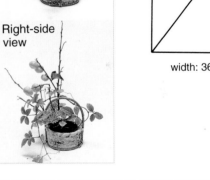

1 DECIDE the direction of basket. Put an inner container in the basket. Set *Gynostemma Pentaphyllum* slanting from the left of the handle, then cascading naturally towards the right.

2 ADD a single tangerine branch extendly towards the right.

3 PLACE the longest branch with tangerines in the center, slanting to the left. Add the remaining branches to the left and front.

4 FILL with chrysanthemums so them brim over towards the left.

Visual illusion

The lower mass of blossoms set up the taller ones, creating a 3D effect.

*Hint
Stems of twin flowers are placed so the lower blossom extends backwards to express depth.

Flowers & Foliage

45 cm (18")

Chrysanthemum in 3 types

Container & Materials

Rectangular basket, 8 cm (3") high, 16 cm (6¼") wide, 10 cm (4") deep
Kenzan (needlepoint holder)
Inner container

Finished Display

Rear view

See the contrast of heights.

Finished Size

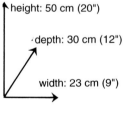

height: 50 cm (20")

depth: 30 cm (12")

width: 23 cm (9")

Method

1	**2**	**3**	**4**

1 CENTER the longest stem of spray mum in inner container upright as shown.

2 ADD the shortest stem of spray mum to the front of the previous stem. Add the remaining mum to the back, slanting slightly to the right.

3 STARTING from the center, fill in the base with pink mum towards the right.

4 FILL in with yellow mums at slightly varying heights.

Reminiscent of autumn

Beautifully gradated hues of autumn depicted here in a small container.

Flowers & Foliage

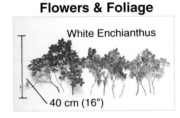

White Enchianthus

40 cm (16")

Container & Materials

Earthen ware, 13 cm (5") high,
18 cm (7") across rim
Kenzan (needlepoint holder)

Finished Size

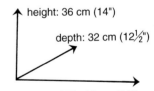

height: 36 cm (14")

depth: 32 cm (12½")

width: 60 cm (24")

Method

1 START from the left side, by slanting the reddest twig from the center of the container towards the left. Add a short twig to the front, then a longer twig behind it.

2 SPREAD to the right, by slanting twigs of greenish leaves towards the left. Do not form symmetrically, and make the right side shorter.

Finished Display

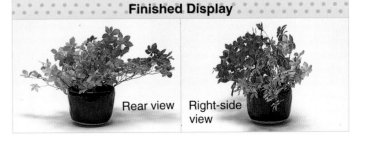

Rear view

Right-side view

✳Hint

Be careful so as not to make a flat surface of leaves. Vary the heights of twigs to present them as naturally as possible.

Mountain in the sunlight

Just a single branch conveys the mood of harvest season.

28

✳Hint

Trim away leaves and berries if necessary so as to balance the heavy heads.

Flowers & Foliage

Japanese winterberry

40 cm (16")

Hosta leaf

Container

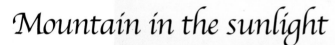

Used whiskey bottle, 22 cm (8½") high, 2 cm (¾") across rim

Finished Size

height: 50 cm (20")

depth: 33 cm (13")

width: 56 cm (22")

Method

1

PLACE a longer branch of Japanese winterberry at a slant so that the best look is achieved.

2

ADD a short branch slanting forward.

3

FILL in the base with hosta leaves. Insert a shorter, wider leaf slanting forward, then a longer leaf behind it, pointing towards upper right.

Finished Display

Left-side view

Moon viewing

This display is a must for a family moon viewing party.

Method

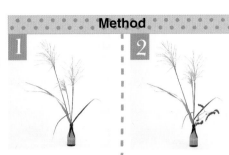

1 SLANT 3 Japanese pampas stalks to create a windblown look, varying the lengths.

2 INSERT smartweed, slanting forward and slightly to the right.

3 GIVE dimension with burnet branches slightly slanting forward and no higher than the pampas heads.

4 FILL in with yellow *Patrinia Scabiosafolia* cut short to spread towards left.

Flowers & Foliage

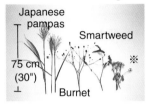

Japanese pampas

Smartweed

75 cm (30")

Burnet

※ *Patrinia Scabiosafolia*

Container

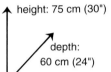

Used bottle, 15 cm (6") high, 2 cm (¾") across rim

Finished Size

height: 75 cm (30")

depth: 60 cm (24")

width: 70 cm (28")

✱Hint
Swordlike leaves of pampas grass need a treatment before being arranged. Cut the edges under water and bury the whole leaves in water until crisp.

Welcoming the autumn

Enjoy the young green burs of chestnut together with a windblown look.

Flowers & Foliage

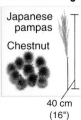

Japanese pampas

Chestnut

40 cm (16")

Containers

A small dish of 3 cm (1⅛") in height and 15 cm (6") across, topped with a smaller dish

Finished Size

height: 38 cm (15")

depth: 25 cm (10")

width: 33 cm (13")

✱Hint
Wear gloves when removing chestnut burs from branches.

Method
LAYER dishes and fill with chestnut burs to look as if some are spilled over.

Brisk autumn day

A harmonious effect is created by the contrasting colors and textures, including the basket.

◆**Variation**
The same style arrangement featuring raspberry branches and pink gerberas.

Method

1

PLACE the longest twig of chestnut slanting forward left, resting at the rim of the container.

2

HOLDING the twig at a slant as shown, and place it in the container.

3

CHECK that both lines extend to opposite directions.

4

ADD the remaining twigs in the center, then on both sides.

5

TAKE a longer stem of cosmos, and set it slanting forward.

6

FINISH by covering the rim of the container with the remaining cosmos facing forward.

Finished Display

Front view

Rear view

Left-side view

Right-side view

Flowers & Foliage

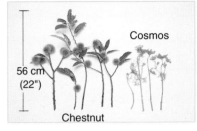

Cosmos

56 cm (22")

Chestnut

Container

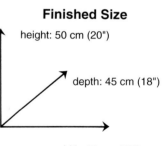

Cone-shaped basket with a stand and inner vase, 25 cm (10") high, 10 cm (4") across rim

Finished Size

height: 50 cm (20")

depth: 45 cm (18")

width: 56 cm (22")

✳Hint

Trim away some leaves to show the chestnut burs effectively. Place cosmos blossoms within the space made between burs.

Streamlines

Dark, thin leaves of dracaena emphasize the delicate tones and shapes of roses arranged in a tall vase.

Method

1 PUT the longest stem of rose a into the left side of the vase, slanting towards the left.

2 SETTLE rose b slanting forward right, almost horizontally.

3 FILL the center space with the remaining roses, each facing forward.

4 ADD a bunch of dracaena leaves flowing naturally to forward left.

5 FINISH off with 3 leaves of dracaena, slightly slanting to the right.

✱Hint
Secure rose stems by crossing each other just inside of the container. Dracaena can be also secured with the crossing.

Finished Display

Front view

Rear view

Left-side view

Right-side view

Check how roses are bowing forward.

Flowers & Foliage

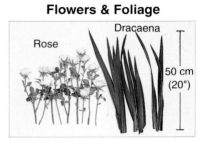

Rose · Dracaena · 50 cm (20")

Container

Cylindrical vase, 23 cm (9") high, 8 cm (3") across

Finished Size

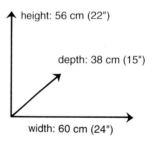

height: 56 cm (22")
depth: 38 cm (15")
width: 60 cm (24")

◆Variation
Bulrush stalks make a sharp statement while miniature roses add delicacy.

33

Femininity

Elegant blossoms of camellia are brimming over a tall vase.

Method

Vary the lengths of camellia stems. Set one by one as if filling a fruit bowl, balancing the hues and slanting forward.

Flowers & Foliage

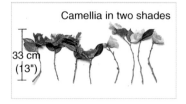

Camellia in two shades

33 cm (13")

Container

Flat vase, 28 cm (11") high, 28 cm (11") wide, 18 cm (7") deep

Finished Size

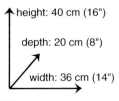

height: 40 cm (16")

depth: 20 cm (8")

width: 36 cm (14")

✳Hint

Combine camellia blossoms showing the best of color and expressions.

Finished Size

height: 23 cm (9")

depth: 36 cm (14")

width: 38 cm (15")

Flowers & Foliage

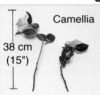

Camellia

38 cm (15")

Container

Earthenware vase, 13 cm (5") high, 5 cm (2") across rim

Simplicity

An elegant and expressive form of simple camellia created by effective trimming.

Method

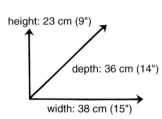

SLANT longer camellia forward left so as to show the best contour. Add short camellia slanting forward right so that the blossom faces up.

Finished Display

Left-side view

◆**Variation**

Different expressions can be made by the shapes of the twigs you choose.

Contrasting texture

The freshness of live plants is emphasized by a withered branch which provides an artistic space.

Method

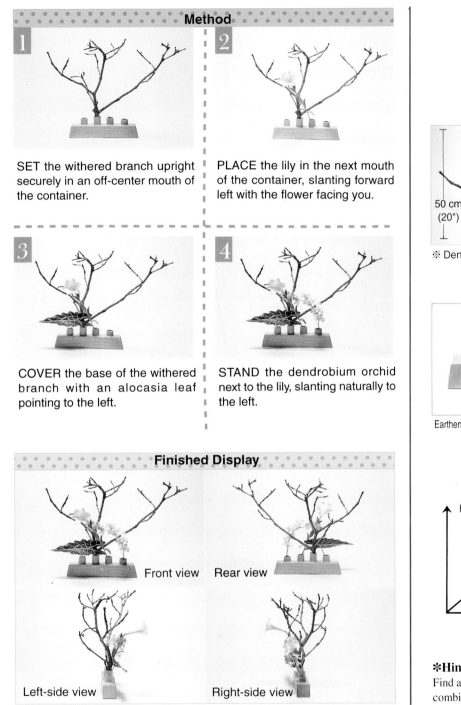

1 SET the withered branch upright securely in an off-center mouth of the container.

2 PLACE the lily in the next mouth of the container, slanting forward left with the flower facing you.

3 COVER the base of the withered branch with an alocasia leaf pointing to the left.

4 STAND the dendrobium orchid next to the lily, slanting naturally to the left.

Finished Display

Front view Rear view

Left-side view Right-side view

Flowers & Foliage

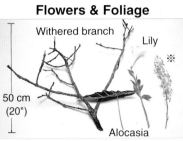

Withered branch Lily

50 cm (20") Alocasia

※ Dendrobium orchid

Container

Earthenware vase, 13 cm (5") high,
36 cm (14") wide,
3 cm (1⅛") across each rim

Finished Size

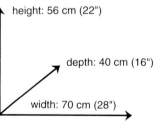

height: 56 cm (22")

depth: 40 cm (16")

width: 70 cm (28")

✻Hint
Find a branch that has a movement, and combine with elegant flowers.

Coincidence

Playful display using withered and forgotten branches enlivened with sheer paper of various shades.

Flowers & Foliage

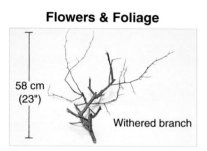

58 cm (23")

Withered branch

Container & Materials

Tin box, 5.5 cm (2¼") high,
 11 cm (4½") wide,
 7.5 cm(2¾") deep
Kenzan (needlepoint holder)
Craft glue, Stub wire
Washi wrapping paper
 (yellow, orange, pink, blue, purple)

Finished Size

height: 56 cm (22")

depth: 40 cm (16")

width: 45 cm (18")

∗Hint
Break thin boughs to make "triangles" and give interesting "shades" to a dark branch.

Method

PLACE a *kenzan* on the bottom of the container, and stand the branch upright, presenting its best side.

How to use paper

1

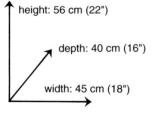

WRAP around branch. Cut paper into 2 cm (¾") strips.

2

APPLY glue to some parts of the branch and wrap it with paper strips covering the parts completely.

Robustness

Simplified version to enjoy a brandnew texture and construction.

Flowers & Foliage

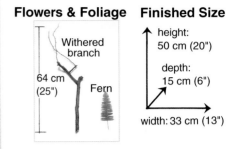

Withered branch

64 cm (25")

Fern

Finished Size

height: 50 cm (20")

depth: 15 cm (6")

width: 33 cm (13")

Container & Materials

Flower pot, 13 cm (5") high, 10 cm (4") across
Kenzan (needlepoint holder)
Craft glue
Washi wrapping paper
(yellow, orange, blue, purple)

3

MAKE triangles. Decide where to make planes, and bend (break) at several points. Secure with wire.

4

CUT out paper slightly longer than the triangles that are made with boughs.

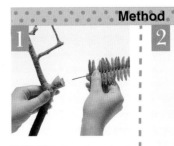

5

APPLY glue to boughs, and attach the triangle paper.

Method

1

INSERT the frond of fern into a cut edge of wrapped branch. If the branch is hard, split a few inches of it using shears.

2

STAND the branch upright in the center of the container.

Charming corner

Yellow blossoms and artistic leaves are set off by a tall blue bottle and a white background.

Finished Display

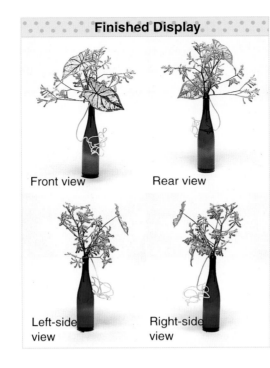

Front view   Rear view

Left-side view   Right-side view

Flowers & Foliage

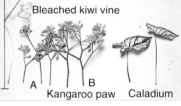

40 cm (16")
Bleached kiwi vine

A   B
Kangaroo paw   Caladium

Method

1 CENTER kangaroo paw (B) upright and securely.

2 ADD kangaroo paw (A) on the left side, slanting almost horizontally. Add remaining kangaroo paw in front of(B), leaning forward.

3 HANG vine, cut edge up, from the upper stem of the kangaroo paw downwards, but not lower than the middle of the bottle.

4 ADD larger caladium leaf at the mouth of the bottle, its tip pointing to left.

5 FINISH with remaining leaf inserted upright, pointing right downwards.

＊Hint
When arranging in a tall, narrow bottle, balance the whole by adding something hanging over.

Container

Wine bottle, 33 cm (13") high, 1.5 cm (½") across rim

Finished Size

height: 60 cm (24")

depth: 40 cm (16")

width: 43 cm (17")

Quiet movement

Soft pink orchid gives a tranquil effect while the ascending line of white vine expresses a movement.

Flowers & Foliage

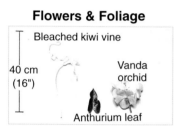

40 cm (16")

Bleached kiwi vine

Vanda orchid

Anthurium leaf

Container

Glass vase, 18 cm (7") high, 20 cm (8") wide

Finished Size

height: 50 cm (20")

depth: 23 cm (9")

width: 23 cm (9")

Method

1

PLACE the orchid flowers on the mouth of the container, towards the right.

2

EXTEND kiwi vine upward from the left side of the mouth, slightly slanting forward.

3

ACCENT with anthurium leaf positioned behind the vine to face you.

Illusion in the water

Speckled leaves look unexpectedly bold when displayed in water because of the lens effect.

Flowers & Foliage

20 cm (8")

Calla lily

Container

Glass vase, 23 cm (9") high, 10 cm (4") across

Finished Size

height: 30 cm (12")

depth: 18 cm (7")

width: 23 cm (9")

✱Hint

Express the beauty of water rather than the floral material. Clean the leaves to keep the water clear.

Method

1 SETTLE 2 leaves under water, tips down, so the top sides are seen.

2 ROLL remaining leaf loosely so that the tip is underneath.

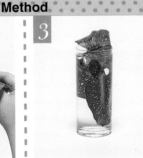

3 HOLDING the stem of the rolled leaf, "bury" it halfway so it is partially seen above the water.

4 FINISH with calla lilies, each pointing in a different direction.

Finished Display

Right-side view

Leaves in the water are settled down with the weight of the flowers.

Nonchalance

A very informal display using a paper bag as the container.

Flowers & Foliage

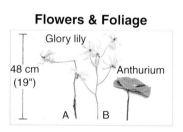

Glory lily

48 cm (19")

Anthurium

A   B

Container & Materials

Paper bag, 20 cm (8") high,
13 cm (5") side, 8 cm (3") deep
Inner container
Stub wire, 40 cm (16") of 2 cm ($\frac{3}{4}$") ribbon

Finished Size

height: 45 cm (18")

depth: 33 cm (13")

width: 48 cm (19")

Finished Display

Rear view

✳Hint
The shiny surface of anthurium echoes the glossy paper.

Method

1

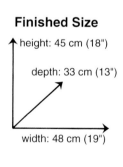

Tie in the middle.

Bind with wire.

Choose a container short enough so as not to peek out from the opening of the bag.

Tie ribbon over the wire.

MAKE the container. Place an inner container inside the paper bag. Join the handles and tie the ribbon into a bow.

2

SLANT glory lily (B), leaning against the left edge of the paper bag. Stand lily (A) upright, next to it so the flower extends towards the left.

3

COVER the lower stems of lilies with anthurium slanting towards forward left, and pointing down right.

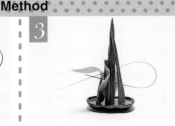

Gradation of Green

Various shapes and shades of foliage harmonize and stand with no support.

Flowers & Foliage

Grasstree

Amaryllis leaf   Hosta leaf   Alstroemeria

35 cm (14")

Container

Oval dish, 3 cm (1⅛") high, 20 cm (8") wide, 13 cm (5") deep

Finished Size

height: 40 cm (16")

depth: 18 cm (7")

width: 48 cm (19")

Finished Display

Rear view

Method

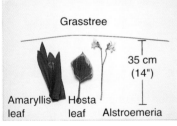

1 THREAD leaves. Over an amaryllis leaf, layer a hosta leaf, then three amaryllis leaves, aligning cut edges. Penetrate the grasstree from the back side, then from the front.

2 STAND threaded leaves in the container, arranging in shapes.

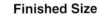

3 CHECK the balance so that the leaves stand securely.

4 ADD alstroemeria to the right side of the hosta by lowering its stem from the back and between grasstree "threads", slanting backwards.

45

SEASONAL CELEBRATIONS

Lay juniper sprigs so as not to look too heavy, and create movement with a curving line of red vine.

Flowers & Foliage

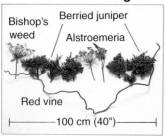

Bishop's weed
Berried juniper
Alstroemeria
Red vine
— 100 cm (40") —

Container & Materials

2 narrow glasses,
   15 cm (6") high,
   3 cm (1 ⅛") across rim
Candle
Candleholder

Finished Size

height: 28 cm (11")
depth: 25 cm (10")
width: 100 cm (40")

Method

CHOOSE a location and position 2 containers apart fro[m] each other. Place the candle. In each glass, place bishop[']s weed and alstroemeria. Arrange juniper sprigs so as to hid[e] the bases of the glasses. Finally lay a piece of vine using th[e] natural curve or by shaping it yourself.

CHRISTMAS

*This magical time attracts people of all ages and nationalities.
Decorating rooms is fun with the special holiday colors of red, green, and white,
counting the days leading up to Christmas.*

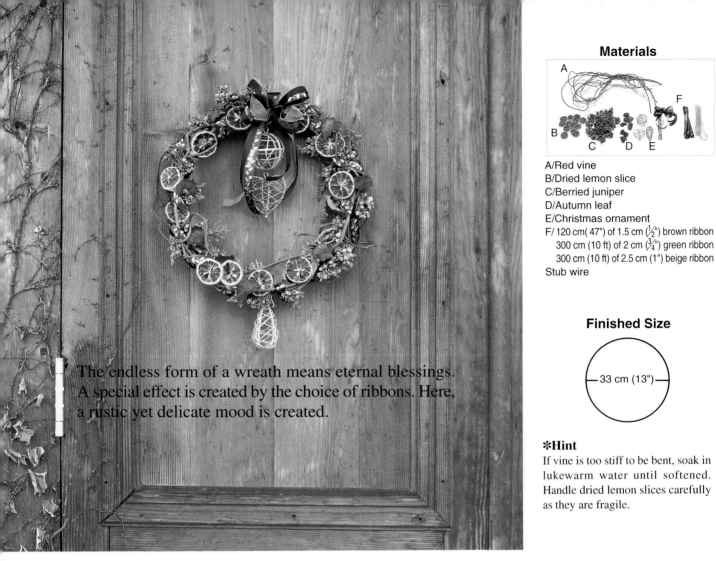

The endless form of a wreath means eternal blessings. A special effect is created by the choice of ribbons. Here, a rustic yet delicate mood is created.

Materials

A/Red vine
B/Dried lemon slice
C/Berried juniper
D/Autumn leaf
E/Christmas ornament
F/ 120 cm (47") of 1.5 cm ($\frac{1}{2}$") brown ribbon
   300 cm (10 ft) of 2 cm ($\frac{3}{4}$") green ribbon
   300 cm (10 ft) of 2.5 cm (1") beige ribbon
Stub wire

Finished Size

— 33 cm (13") —

*Hint

If vine is too stiff to be bent, soak in lukewarm water until softened. Handle dried lemon slices carefully as they are fragile.

Method

1 FORM a ring. Hold several pieces of vine, varying each end, and twine them into a ring of 25 cm (10") at inner diameter.

2 PUSH the ends of the vine into the ring to finish.

3 BIND the ring with green ribbon layered on beige ribbon. Tie the ends.

4 MAKE a bow with beige, green, and brown ribbons. Wire onto the wreath.

5 ATTACH ornaments using wire, under the bow and bottom of the wreath.

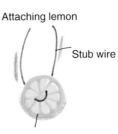

6 INSERT berried juniper twigs evenly into vines. Attach dried lemon slices wired as shown at right.

Attaching lemon

Stub wire

Lemon

7 FINISH with autumn leaves by inserting each into vines after securing the wreath in the place.

Spread joy over the table, and highlight the candle with red poinsettia.

Materials

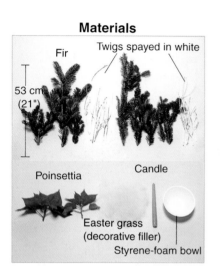

Fir

Twigs spayed in white

53 cm (21")

Poinsettia

Candle

Easter grass (decorative filler)

Styrene-foam bowl

Container

Glass bowl, 8 cm (3") high, 28 cm (11") across

Finished Size

height: 33 cm (13")

depth: 60 cm (24")

width: 120 cm (47")

✳Hint
Surround the candle with angel's hair, resembling snow.

1

MAKE cnadleholder. Using a craft knife, cut an X into the center of styrene-foam bowl.

2

THRUST the candle at a right angle.

3

PLACE the candleholder in the center of container.

4

FILL the container with Easter grass so as to conceal the base of candleholder, forming a hemisphere.

5

PLACE the poinsettia on the left and right sides of the candle.

6

POSITION on a table, and finish with sprigs of fir and white twigs, arranged to extend both sides.

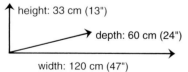

Brighten every corner with interesting vines of green brier and red berries.

Flowers & Materials

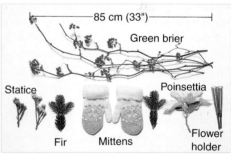

85 cm (33")

Green brier

Statice

Fir   Mittens

Poinsettia

Flower holder

Pushpins

Method

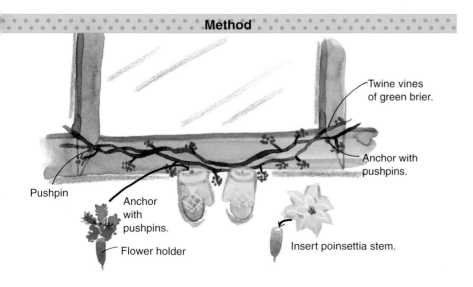

Twine vines of green brier.

Anchor with pushpins.

Pushpin

Anchor with pushpins.

Flower holder

Insert poinsettia stem.

Finished Size

height: 28 cm (11")

width: size of window

❋Hint

If a flower holder is unavailable, use any small, lightweight bottles.

49

Flowers & Materials

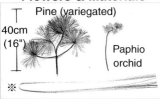

Pine (variegated)

40cm (16")

Paphio orchid

※ *Mizuhiki* paper cord, in gold/silver

Container

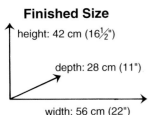

Stem vase, 13 cm (5") high,
2.5 cm (1") across rim

Finished Size

height: 42 cm (16½")

depth: 28 cm (11")

width: 56 cm (22")

✳Hint

Focus on achieving a balance above the tiny vase. Make a flat surface with a strand of *mizuhiki* cords, and form a smooth circle to symbolize harmony.

Mizuhiki cord adds to a formal atmosphere.

NEW YEAR HOLIDAY

As an evergreen tree, pine represents eternal life and is especially favored for the New Year's arrangements that welcome happiness.

Method

1 PLACE pine slightly slanting towards the right, presenting the best of its shape.

2 TIE *mizuhiki* cords onto the pine stem, just above the container. Hold ends in each hand, and make a circle of 15 cm (6") diameter, then form a smaller circle above it.

3 CHECKING the overall balance, tie the *mizuhiki* loosely behind the pine. Let the golden ends flow towards left, and the silver ends fall behind.

4 ADD orchid to the center, slanting forward to finish.

Fresh, cut bamboo stalk makes a popular container for the New Year. This simplified pair of arrangements shows a horizontal and vertical contrast.

Flowers & Foliage

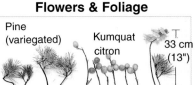

Pine (variegated)

Kumquat citron

33 cm (13")

Phalaenopsis orchid

Containers & Materials

2 cut bamboo cylinders, 13 cm (5") and 14 cm (5½") in height
2 *kenzans* (needlepoint holders)

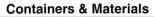

Method

1 POSITION containers, and place pine sprigs. Left: Extend pine to both sides. Right: Slant shorter sprigs slightly forward.

2 PLACE kumquat stems and orchid. Left: Add kumquat stems one by one, at varying heights. Right: Stand orchid upright to finish.

Finished Size

[Left]
height: 30 cm (12")
depth: 13 cm (5")
width: 40 cm (16")

[Right]
height: 38 cm (15")
depth: 13 cm (5")
width: 13 cm (5")

Check the balance when placing the kumquat stems since the fruit is heavy. Show the rising line of orchid.

51

A single twig and a simple wreath are effectively displayed in the hope of good days to come.

Flowers & Foliage

Pine (variegated)
Paphio orchid
Chloranthus glaber
15 cm (6")

Containers & Materials

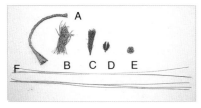

Wooden measure (180 ml)
Kenzan (needlepoint holder), Stub wire

Materials for Rope Wreath

A/Straw rope B/Ear of rice
C/Young pine D/Fan ornament
E/Pine cone
F/*Mizuhiki* cord (gold and red)

Finished Size

height: 27 cm (17")
depth: 15 cm (6")
width: 33 cm (13")
[Measure]

width: 23 cm (9")
10 cm (4")
height: 18 cm (7")
[Wreath]

Method

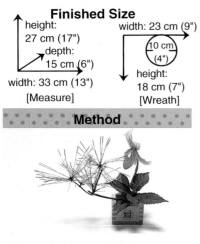

Place the *kenzan* in the measure. Using the natural shape, slant the pine twig to the right almost horizontally. Stand orchid upright in the center, then add the Chloranthus glabor to the front.

52

Sacred Rope Wreath

1

CROSS ends of the sacred straw rope. Add the pine and the ear of rice on the joint, and bind with wire 4-5 times. Wind red and white *mizuhiki* cords to cover the wire, and twist at the back.

2

ATTACH the pine cone by threading it with stub wire and twisting the ends at the back.

3

ATTACH the fan using the wire ends at the back so as to show the pine cone effectively.

4

Front view of the finished wreath.

5

Rear view of the finished wreath. Attach a loop of wire for hanging to the back side.

✳Hint

Try to make the most of a tiny container and a few floral materials.

Express joy on a lacquered serving tray of *sake*.

Flowers & Foliage

Pine

Daffodil

28 cm (11")

Anthurium

Materials

Bamboo cylinder
Mizuhiki cord (gold/silver)
Washi paper (red and white)

Containers

Flat lacquerware plate, 15 cm (6") across
Lacquerware tray, 40 cm (16") across

Finished Size

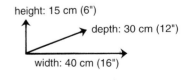

height: 15 cm (6")

depth: 30 cm (12")

width: 40 cm (16")

*Hint

Do not put too much material on the tray. Leave some room to give a spacious impression.

Method

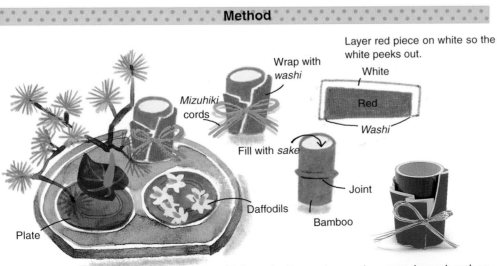

Wrap with *washi*

Mizuhiki cords

Plate

Daffodils

Layer red piece on white so the white peeks out.

White

Red

Washi

Fill with *sake*

Joint

Bamboo

Make a festive *sake* cup by wrapping a bamboo piece with layered *washi* and tie a bow with gold and silver cords.

Decorate the door with a freestyle display using symbolic materials for the New Year.

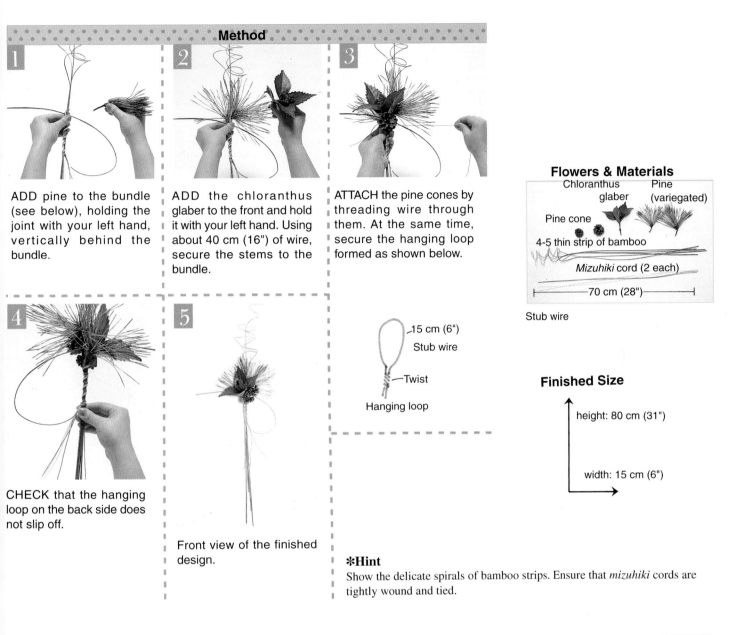

Method

1 ADD pine to the bundle (see below), holding the joint with your left hand, vertically behind the bundle.

2 ADD the chloranthus glaber to the front and hold it with your left hand. Using about 40 cm (16") of wire, secure the stems to the bundle.

3 ATTACH the pine cones by threading wire through them. At the same time, secure the hanging loop formed as shown below.

4 CHECK that the hanging loop on the back side does not slip off.

5 Front view of the finished design.

15 cm (6")
Stub wire
Twist
Hanging loop

Flowers & Materials

Chloranthus glaber
Pine (variegated)
Pine cone
4-5 thin strip of bamboo
Mizuhiki cord (2 each)
70 cm (28")
Stub wire

Finished Size

height: 80 cm (31")

width: 15 cm (6")

✳Hint
Show the delicate spirals of bamboo strips. Ensure that *mizuhiki* cords are tightly wound and tied.

How to bind bamboo strips with *Mizuhiki* cords

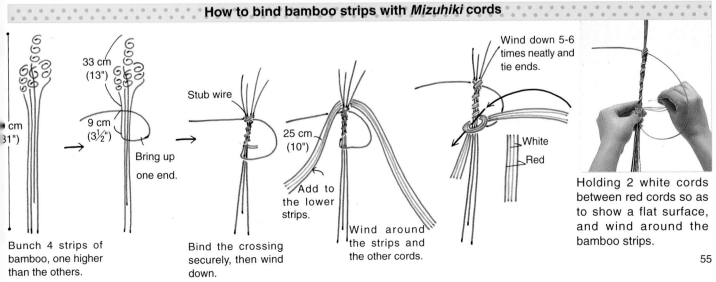

33 cm (13")

9 cm (3½")
Bring up one end.

cm (31")

Bunch 4 strips of bamboo, one higher than the others.

Stub wire

Bind the crossing securely, then wind down.

25 cm (10")
Add to the lower strips.

Wind around the strips and the other cords.

Wind down 5-6 times neatly and tie ends.

White
Red

Holding 2 white cords between red cords so as to show a flat surface, and wind around the bamboo strips.

55

The straight lines of peach branches emphasize the gentle lines of spirea that expresses femininity.

DOLL FESTIVAL

Early in March, wishes are made so that little girls will grow up to be healthy and affectionate. The combination of peach and rapeseed blossoms is a must along with the traditional doll set.

Method

1 CHOOSE 2 longer branches of peach. Place them in the center of the container so they stretch freely to the left and right.

2 ADD remaining peach twigs to the center, slanting slightly forward, tops spreading widely.

3 ADD spirea. Set the longest branch behind the peach so it extends forward left.

4 ADD remaining spirea behind, naturally slanting forward.

Flowers brimming out from a fancy box to herald the spring.

Flowers & Foliage

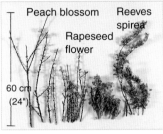

Peach blossom   Reeves spirea

Rapeseed flower

60 cm (24")

Container & Materials

Glassware, 5 cm (2") high,
30 cm (12") across
Kenzan (needlepoint holder)

Finished Size

height: 64 cm (25")

depth: 45 cm (18")

width: 75 cm (30")

Flowers & Foliage

Peach blossom

48 cm (19")

Larkspur blue spray

Container & Materials

Covered box, 10 cm (4") high,
15 cm (6") wide, 8 cm (3") deep
Inner container
Kenzan (needlepoint holder)

Finished Size

height: 30 cm (12")

depth: 33 cm (13")

width: 53 cm (21")

Method

SET peach branches as if they are growing up boldly.

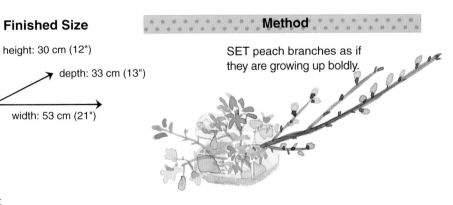

SLANT larkspur blue spray forward, almost horizontally.

5

FINISH with rapeseed flowers placed to hide the base of arrangement, slanting forward.

✻Hint
Express the linear beauty of peach, studded with dreamy pink buds.

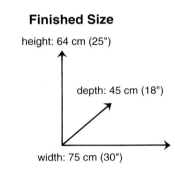

BOY'S DAY

On the 5th of May when every tree starts sprouting out, parents display carp streamers in the yard while they enjoy ikebana featuring Japanese irises inside. The sword-like, soaring leaves of iris symbolize strength for boys.

Sweetflag leaves are usually placed upright. However, this arrangement adopts a slant in order to give lightness in contrast with voluminous base that stretches from right to left.

Method

1 SET longest maple branch at the center of the container. Slant towards front left.

2 ADD remaining maple twigs to form a dense "shrub" covering the rim of the container.

3 STAND sweetflag leaves together behind the maple. Slant slightly forward.

4 PLACE clematis on the right, slanting forward right.

Flowers & Foliage

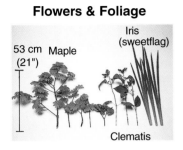

53 cm (21") Maple

Iris (sweetflag)

Clematis

Container & Materials

Earthenware, 11 cm (4½") high,
14 cm (5½") wide,
10 cm (4") deep
Kenzan (needlepoint holder)

Finished Size

height: 50 cm (20")

depth: 28 cm (11")

width: 40 cm (16")

Finished Display

Right-side view

This simplified, yet expressive arrangement uses distinctive lines.

Flowers & Foliage

Maple
60 cm (24")

Iris (sweetflag)

Lapeirousia

Container

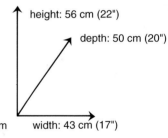

Vase, 15 cm (6") high,
3 cm (1⅛") across rim

Finished Size

height: 56 cm (22")

depth: 50 cm (20")

width: 43 cm (17")

✱Hint

Narrow the width of arrangement just above the rim of vase, and express swift movements with the stems of lapeirousia.

Method

1	2	3

1 PLACE maple slanting forward left almost horizontally.

2 PLACE sweetflag leaves so they rise slightly to the right, and give strength and height.

3 ADD natural flowing lines of lapeirousia one by one, from behind the sweetflag.

STAR FESTIVAL

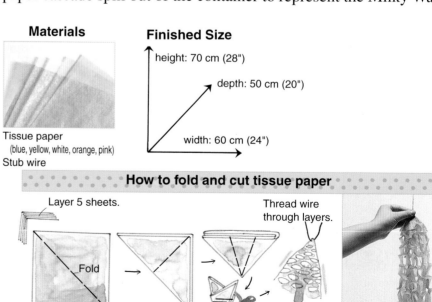

The Star Festival is celebrated on the 7th of July. According to a legend, Vega, Weaver Princess and Altair, Cowboy, are allowed to cross the Milky Way, and meet on this special night of the year. We decorate bamboos with ornaments and colorful slips of paper on which we write down our wishes.

Let tissue paper cascade spill out of the container to represent the Milky Way.

Flowers & Foliage

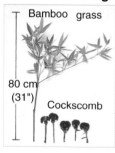

Bamboo grass

80 cm (31")

Cockscomb

Container

Wine bottle, 23 cm (9") high, 1.5 cm (½") across rim
Glassware, 10cm (4") high, 1.5 cm (½") across rim

Materials

Tissue paper
(blue, yellow, white, orange, pink)
Stub wire

Finished Size

height: 70 cm (28")

depth: 50 cm (20")

width: 60 cm (24")

How to fold and cut tissue paper

Layer 5 sheets.

Fold

45 cm (18")

Make slits into both sides.

Thread wire through layers.

Pull and separate with hand.

Method

1

STAND bamboo grass upright in the center.

2

HANG the folded paper on the cut edge of bamboo. Let it flow toward left and widen at the bottom.

3

PLACE cockscomb in the small container, at varying heights.

4

POSITION two containers in place for a finished arrangement.

Fresh green hues of bamboo are enriched with cute, fuchsia flowers that look as if they are still growing up.

Method

1

STAND bamboo upright and securely in the center of container.

2

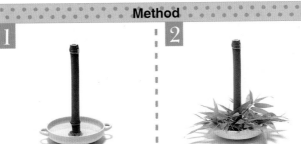

FILL the container with bamboo leaves. Let the leaves soak in water to prevent curling.

3

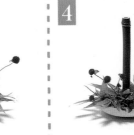

ACCENT with a long globe amaranth, slanting to the right.

4

FINISH with more globe amaranth placed behind, at the left and front of the bamboo stalk, but not on the right.

Flowers & Foliage

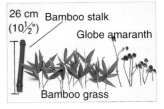

26 cm (10½") Bamboo stalk
Globe amaranth
Bamboo grass

Container

Earthenware casserole, 2.5 cm (1") high, 15 cm (6") across
Kenzan (needlepoint holder)

Finished Size

height: 30 cm (12")

depth: 30 cm (12")

width: 33 cm (13")

SPECIAL OCCASIONS

An arrangement of flowers on the dinner table can evoke a special atmosphere to welcome your guests. From a group of tiny compositions to a grand display, there are endless possibilities, and it's a good chance to show your sense and ideas.

Consider the overall effect when selecting colors and proportions so that complement each other.

Flowers & Foliage

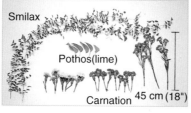

Smilax

Pothos(lime)

Carnation 45 cm (18")

Containers & Materials

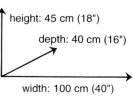

Stem vase, 13 cm (8") high, 2.5 cm(1") across rim
Coffee cup, 6.5 cm (2½") high, 7 cm (2¾") across rim
Glasses, each 8 cm (3") high, 5.5 cm (2¼") across
Candles (3 red, 2 green, 1 yellow)

Finished Size

height: 45 cm (18")

depth: 40 cm (16")

width: 100 cm (40")

Method

1 POSITION 4 containers, the stem vase on the very left. Place carnations of varied lengths in the stem vase so as to make a fanned design.

2 FILL coffee cup with pothos leaves. Place carnations of each color in a dome shape in glasses.

3 ADD a sprig of smilax to the Right side of the vase, and form a circle on the table, letting the tip flow behind the vase.

4 FINISH with the other smilax sprig added to the left side of the vase. Let the remainder run behind the next container, then to the front.

A single stem of flowers is most beautifully shown in this joyful arrangement.

❋Hint

Create a delicate movement with colored wire.

Colored wire

Bend to fit in the container.

Flowers & Materials

Dendrobium orchid

45 cm (18")

Baby's breath

Colored fine wire
(20 pcs. each blue and silver, 12 pcs. red)

Container

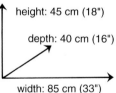

Glass vase, 20 cm (8") high,
6 cm (2¼") across rim

Finished Size

height: 45 cm (18")

depth: 40 cm (16")

width: 85 cm (33")

Method

1

PREPARE colored wire. Holding the wires in both hands, join the ends just above the container.

2

TURN 90° so the circles face to sides, and place in the container. Holding the base of wire in one hand, fan out each piece with the other hand.

3

Completed design of colored wire.

4

FILL the space between wire with baby's breath, placing one by one into a dome shape.

5

PLACE orchid slanting to flow naturally towards left.

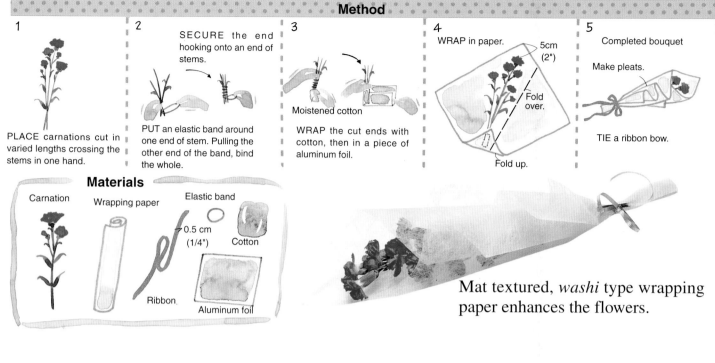

1

PLACE carnations cut in varied lengths crossing the stems in one hand.

2

SECURE the end hooking onto an end of stems.

PUT an elastic band around one end of stem. Pulling the other end of the band, bind the whole.

3

Moistened cotton

WRAP the cut ends with cotton, then in a piece of aluminum foil.

4

WRAP in paper.

5cm (2")

Fold over.

Fold up.

5

Completed bouquet

Make pleats.

TIE a ribbon bow.

Materials

Carnation

Wrapping paper

Elastic band

0.5 cm (1/4")

Cotton

Ribbon

Aluminum foil

Mat textured, *washi* type wrapping paper enhances the flowers.

GIFTS OF FLOWERS

Add bold leaves to a bunch of flowers for a sophisticated look.

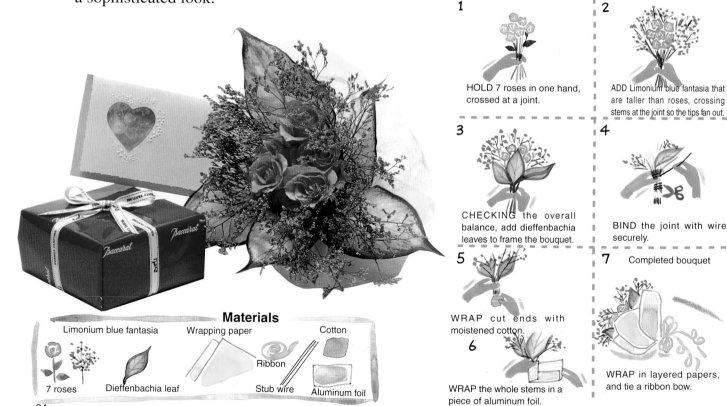

Materials

Limonium blue fantasia

Wrapping paper

Cotton

Ribbon

7 roses

Dieffenbachia leaf

Stub wire

Aluminum foil

1

HOLD 7 roses in one hand, crossed at a joint.

2

ADD Limonium blue fantasia that are taller than roses, crossing stems at the joint so the tips fan out.

3

CHECKING the overall balance, add dieffenbachia leaves to frame the bouquet.

4

BIND the joint with wire securely.

5

WRAP cut ends with moistened cotton.

6

WRAP the whole stems in a piece of aluminum foil.

7

Completed bouquet

WRAP in layered papers, and tie a ribbon bow.

IKEBANA CONTAINERS

Ikebana is complete only if arranged in an appropriate container. To select one that will harmonize with the floral arrangement, consider the shape, color, size and texture of the container.

Glass container

The clarity and freshness of glass create a mood appropriate for any season or style. Since glass containers expose the water within, you should consider how immersed stems will look through the glass.

Tall vase

The most practical tall vase is likely a cylinder or prism, about 30 cm-40 cm (12"-16") high, and 10 cm-15 cm (4"-6") wide.

Pot

Choose a heavy, stable pot with a small opening. When arranging, turn the pot around and check the best side in order to show the best of the arrangement.

Bowl

Look around your house for anything that could be used as a container to match your arrangement.

Compote

Compote-shaped containers are used specially for a modern arrangement or when a certain height is required.

Basket

Bamboo or rattan baskets go very well with floral materials because both are made of natural plants. Arrangements in woven containers create a rustic, warm impression. Natural bamboo colanders complement wild flowers picked in the field or in your garden. Be sure the water container is stable in the basket.

Suiban (shallow container)

Suiban come in various shapes, such as round, oval, rectangular, or triangular. One that has about a 30 cm (12") diameter and a 4-5 cm (1½"- 2") height is recommended.

BASIC TECHNIQUES OF IKEBANA

CHOOSING FLORAL MATERIALS

Although there are no rules or taboos when choosing floral materials, it seems that some combinations are more harmonious than others. For beginners, a combination of branches and flowers is highly recommended. The strength of branches affects and complements the fragile beauty of flowers and creates an unexpected effect which could never be achieved if either of them are used alone. Sometimes flowers and foliage are bent to create streamlines. The methods are given at the bottom of this page, but a considerable amount of practice is necessary especially for beginners.

CUTTING METHODS

Cut away any leaves or twigs that are damaged, broken or too dense and define the stem lines clearly. If necessary, straighten a curved stem or bend a straight stem before cutting to required length.

●Cutting a flower stem

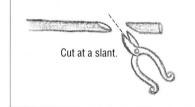

Cut at the right angle.

Cut flowers quickly at the right angle. Thin stems can be cut using the tips of the scissors whereas thicker stems can be easily cut if placed well inside the blades. When cutting a hollow stalk of flowers such as calla lily or daffodil, catch the stalk between the blades of the scissors, and rotate the stalk as you cut. Be careful not to apply too much pressure on blades to avoid crushing the tissue of the stem.

●Cutting a branch

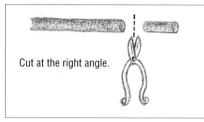

Cut at a slant.

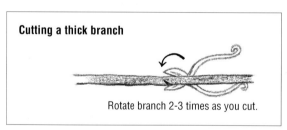

Cutting a thick branch

Rotate branch 2-3 times as you cut.

Cut branches diagonally so that the edges can be easily inserted in *kenzan*(needlepoint holder) or pushed against the inner wall of the vase. Open the scissor handles wide, put the branch well inside the blades at an angle, and cut off.

When the branch is too thick to cut with a single motion of the scissors, catch it well inside the blades and cut as far as you can. Remove scissors and repeat the same motion until the stem is completely cut. Another way of cutting a thick branch is to rotate it as you cut the outside, and then breaking it with both hands. A small saw may come in useful for cutting very thick branches.

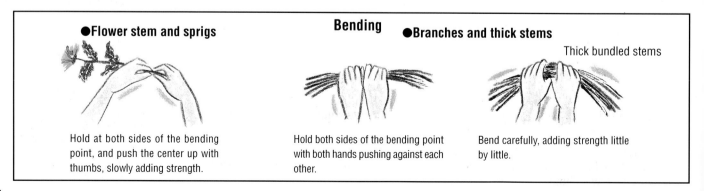

Bending

●Flower stem and sprigs

Hold at both sides of the bending point, and push the center up with thumbs, slowly adding strength.

●Branches and thick stems

Thick bundled stems

Hold both sides of the bending point with both hands pushing against each other.

Bend carefully, adding strength little by little.

CONDITIONING METHODS

Flowers tend to wilt prematurely if cut and exposed to the air for some time. There are several traditional devices to help the stem ends absorb water. Before giving any special treatment, it is essential to cut the stems deep under water.

1 Cutting under water

This is the basic preservation method to increase water intake. Cut the stems deep under water, and the pressure allows the water to be drawn up easily. Every flower must be cut this way before being treated in any of the following methods.

Good for:
All plants except lotus and other water plants

2 Hot water treatment

Some flowers such as peony or amaranth tend to wither quickly. Dip cut ends of flowers into hot water for 1-2 minutes and then into cold water immediately. The difference in temperature hastens water absorption. Baby's breath in winter lasts longer with this treatment.

Good for:
Globe amaranth, Patrinia scabiosafollia, Lady's mantle, Hollyhock, Amaranth, Great burnet, Baby's breath, Peony, Scotch broom, Cockscomb

3 Charring

Wrap the blossoms and leaves in wet newspaper and char the cut ends over direct fire. Burn until the ends glow red, for 1-2 minutes, then dip into cold water immediately.

Good for:
Rose, Miniature rose, Spray mum, Croton, Poinsettia, Peach blossom

4 Crushing

Hard, fibrous stems can be conditioned using this method. Using the side of a pair of closed scissors, crush the ends about 5 cm (2"). Thinner stems such as clematis can be crushed between your teeth. Leave the stems in water before arranging. If using a *kenzan*, cut away some of the crushed end.

Good for:
Reeves spirea, Balloonflower

5 Breaking

Hard and fibrous flowers such as chrysanthemum can be easily broken under water. This enlarges the surface area of the stem and speeds water intake.

Good for:
Chrysanthemum, Spray mum

6 Splitting

Holding the branch with your hand, with the diagonally cut end up, make a cross cut quickly. This method also enlarges the surface area of the stem end and speeds water intake.

Good for:
Japanese maholia, Camellia, Flowering quince, Maple

Chemical Treatments

Wipe the cut edges of floral material dry before applying the chemicals. This promotes absorption of chemicals.

7 Mint oil

This is used to disinfect the cut edges. Dip the end into mint oil before arranging in the container. The stem end of clematis should be crushed with a hammer or scissors before dipping.

Good for:
Caladium, Mountain laurel, Blazing-star, Clematis, Hosta

8 Vinegar

Vinegar is used for its sterilizing effect on plants. Cut the stem end and immediately dip into vinegar before arranging.

Good for:
Bamboo, Japanese pumpas, Shepherd's purse, Foxtil, Bamnoo grass, Begonia, Aster

9 Alcohol

Add *sake* or whisky to the water in the container after arranging.

Good for:
Smokegrass, Wisteria, Blazing-star

10 Salt

Salt is especially effective for flowers in bloom from summer to autumn. The stem end should be crushed before being rubbed with salt.

Good for:
Balloonflower, Sunflower, Great burnet, Caladium, Bird's nest fern, Bamboo

11 Plant food

Flowers which have short life spans such as a few days will last a week by adding plant food available at flower shops or garden centers.

Good for:
All flowers and foliage

FIXING TECHNIQUES

Securing method differs greatly depending on the arranging style and the types of container.

Fixing onto *kenzan*

●Thin stems

Push the stem end into the spikes. Push until the cut end rests on the bottom of *kenzan*. Slant the stem, if preferred, after this securing procedure. If slanting low, push the end onto the spikes with enough strength to secure the side of the stem. The following are the techniques of fixing flowers according to the pliability and thickness of the stems.

Capping

1 If the stem is sturdy but too thin to be secured in *kenzan*, it is often reinforced by capping with a thicker stem in hand.

2 Cut 2-3 cm(3/4"-1⅛") long piece from a thicker stem, and insert the thin stem into this supporting cap.

Binding	**Reinforcing: A**	**Reinforcing: B**	**Folding stems**	**Supporting**
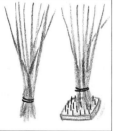	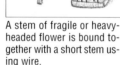	2.5 cm (1") 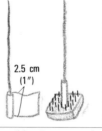		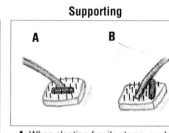
Very thin stems can be bound together using wire so as to add thickness.	A stem of fragile or heavy-headed flower is bound together with a short stem using wire.	Very thin stems can be wrapped with paper so as to add thickness.	If the stem is too thin to be secured in *kenzan*, bend the end to for a "V" and insert into spikes.	**A**: When slanting fragile stems, push a small piece of branch horizontally into *kenzan*, then place the stem against it. **B**: Stand a small piece of branch on *kenzan* and rest the thin stem on it.

●Branches

Try to push branches into the spaces between the spikes rather than into the spikes themselves. Cut the stem so the edge is slightly wider than the interval between the spikes.

When slanting the stem, cut the edge at a slant so the longer bark remains on the slanting side. Push the stem upright into *kenzan*, and carefully slant it towards the longer side. Make sure that this side is secured firmly.

Arranging without *kenzan*

●Cross-bar fixture (fixed in vase)

From a sturdy yet pliable twig, cut two pieces that are slightly longer than the diameter of the vase.

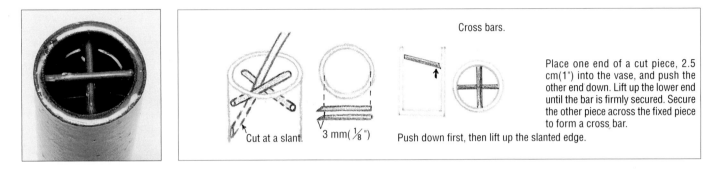

Cross bars.

Cut at a slant.

3 mm(⅛")

Push down first, then lift up the slanted edge.

Place one end of a cut piece, 2.5 cm(1") into the vase, and push the other end down. Lift up the lower end until the bar is firmly secured. Secure the other piece across the fixed piece to form a cross bar.

●Vertical bar fixture (fixed on material)

When a floral material is heavy-headed and does not stay at a desired angle, a slit piece of branch can be used to support it in place. Cut out a piece slightly shorter than the diameter of the vase. Split one end deep enough to hold the material at the desired height. Split the material at the bottom and interlock it with the supporting stalk in the vase. This way the material is secured at three points: (**a**) the rim of the vase, (**b**) the interlocking point, and (**c**) the inner wall of the vase. If the material is too thin to split, thrust it into the slit.

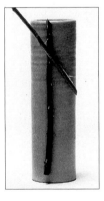

1 Cut the supporting stalk a little shorter than the height of the vase. Split the top end to the desired depth.

2 It may be necessary to split the end slightly deeper than the interlocking point.

3 Slit the floral material and interlock it with the supporting stalk.

4 Cut the bottom edges of the floral material flush with the inner wall of the vase.

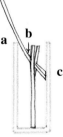

a   b

c

●Direct fixing

The branch rests only at two points of the vase: the rim and the inner wall of the vase.

Techniques for direct fixing

Breaking

Cutting at a slant

Angle depends on the slant.

Slitting

Bending

IKEBANA UTENSILS

Scissors

There are several kinds of scissors or shears specially made for ikebana. Choose whichever is easy for you to handle. When cutting a branch, place the cutting point between the blades of scissors as deep as possible, and grasp firmly. When cutting thicker branches, split the end deep enough to reach the cutting point. Rub oil on the blades after every use to prevent them from rusting.

Handling scissors

1 Hold the upper hanndle between your thumb and palm, the lower handle with your fingers.

2 Hold tightly, without putting any fingers between the handles.

Kenzan

Kenzan, or a needlepoint holders, come in various shapes and sizes. They can hold the materials at any angle and allow them to be rearranged many times. Choose a heavy one with as many as spikes possible.

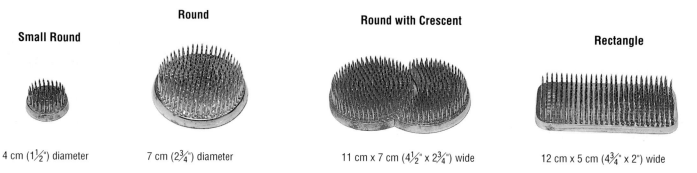

Small Round

Round

Round with Crescent

Rectangle

4 cm (1½") diameter

7 cm (2¾") diameter

11 cm x 7 cm (4½" x 2¾") wide

12 cm x 5 cm (4¾" x 2") wide

Kenzan repairer

Hard or thick branches may bend the spikes of a *kenzan*. A needle repairer is the best tool to straighten the bent spikes.

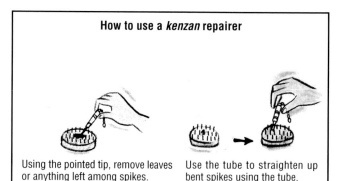

How to use a *kenzan* repairer

Using the pointed tip, remove leaves or anything left among spikes.

Use the tube to straighten up bent spikes using the tube.

BASIC TECHNIQUES OF IKEBANA

Saw

When the branches are too thick or too hard to cut with scissors, a tiny saw might come in handy. A portable folding saw made especially for ikebana is very convenient when you go outdoors for branch hunting.

Stub wire

Thin wires are used to bind floral materials into a secured style. There are straight and rolled lengths of wire in various thicknesses and colors. Green- or brown-colored type is most versatile. Choose #30 wire of the matching color.

Bowl

A medium-sized, deep bowl or any appropriate container is used when cutting plants under water so that they will stay fresh longer.

Water spray

Spray water over the finished arrangement and wash off dirt or dust on the leaves. For a floral display placed in a dry area or in an air-conditioned room, it is essential to give extra water because the flowers absorb moisture through the petals and leaves as well as up through the stem. Spray generous amount of mist occasionally to prevent dryness.

Chicken net

Rolled chicken net can easily hold numbers of thick stems such as gladiolus or stock.

Pebbles

Varieties of pebbles and marbles are used to hide and give weight to a *kenzan*. Choose pebbles that complement the color of flowers.

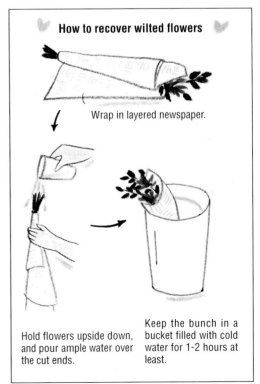

How to recover wilted flowers

Wrap in layered newspaper.

Hold flowers upside down, and pour ample water over the cut ends.

Keep the bunch in a bucket filled with cold water for 1-2 hours at least.

Index